Poetry by

Steve Wheeler

First published by
Wheelsong Books
4 Willow Close, Plymouth PL3 6EY,
United Kingdom

© Steve Wheeler, 2021

Cover design © Steve Wheeler, 2021

First published in 2021

Print ISBN 979-8-45386-796-7

Dedicated to my fellow poets
and Absolutely Poetry

Of all the lives
in all the world
You had to
walk into mine

Inside

RITE

This book just cost me most of my best poems. Plenty of my recent ones anyway. I was saving them for a rainy day, and guess what? It rained continually for two weeks.

Most of these poems are previously unpublished. They are the concrete versions of my thoughts on faith, love and the life we live together on this planet. The title? Well, I could easily have called it Faith and Love, but that would be a little boring and definitely too predictable.

So I called it RITE. A rite is an established, ceremonial, usually religious, act. I think have the right to use the word rite as the title for this poetry book, because to write is an act of ceremony, and in my case, it's definitely an act of expressing my faith. I think this is my most ambitious collection to date.

I hope you enjoy it.

Steve Wheeler
Plymouth
September 2021

Music of the Spheres

Jupiter jumps
and Uranus swings
Saturn's wearing
all its rings
Mars grooves
and Venus sings
Mercury dresses up
with wings
Earth takes to the floor
with the Moon
Moving to the rhythm
of the old Nep-tune

(NB: Other planets are available)

You only ever quote from Friends

These days you only quote from Friends;
what happened to your Nietzsche?
The philosophy of Chandler Bing
has become a regular feature

The monologues of Monica
and the rhetoric of Rachel
imbue your conversation
at the expense of Marx and Hegel.

From the theory of Unagi,
to the Smelly Cat conjecture,
and the "how you doin'?" thesis,
they're all found in your lecture.

Could I be more bored of Joey?
I've had my fill of Phoebe Buffay,
and listening to Ross is dull, dull, dull
he has nothing profound to say.

There's only one Friends philosophy
that rings out strong and true;
so no matter what the future holds,
you know: I'll be there for you.

Argent

Rings made out of argent
cut to shape by golden shears
Face masks for the ardent
worn throughout pandemic years
We measure hours with tea spoons
as we transgress dark frontiers
The days pass inexorably
in the movement of the spheres
playing out our normal lives
'til the tragic interferes
The harshest noise of all
must be the grinding of the gears
So deafening, the silence
that assails our listening ears
resounding as the bulwark
of our freedom disappears
Will we ever find the means
to exorcise our fears?
Should we ever wipe away
the tracking of our tears?
The days pass in procession
like the music of the spheres
Rings made out of argent
cut to shape by golden shears

Epic Lines

I want to write those epic lines
I want to be a sign of the times
send my bars and verses spinning
give the sign that I am winning
I want to pen some awesome ink
the kind that really makes you think
I want my words to heart inspire
to run you down to the final wire
I hope my words will be eternal
to stand apart from the dark infernal
to stand out high above the crowd
to shout to yell to scream out loud
I'm not ashamed to bare my soul
to take the truth and speak it whole
in unadulterated form
To weather out the perfect storm
I want to write those epic lines
that make you forget the tie that binds
to make you remember who you are
a burning, shining, radiant star

This Bed

this bed becomes
the landscape
of my dreams
my blankets
form the Atlas
of my years
this mattress
holds the rhythm
of my sleep
while my pillow
cries a thousand
lonely tears

Harmful Love

Oh, harmful love
you will not set me free
Destructive love
is there no hope for me?
I try and run,
I try to hide my fretful face
but liberty has
disappeared without a trace

I run from you
and to my freedom flee
But I can never
find the exit key
Caught in the
courtyard of anxiety
Oh, harmful love
I fight you constantly

Inscriptions

On an ancient palace wall
mystery words were slowly scrawled.
The king watched their inscription
but he failed in his translation.
Then a prophet saw the sight
and through mists he shone a light
giving warnings of invasion,
and of judgement and salvation.

Words written in the dirt,
contained a message to assert.
Though many watched the scene
few could see what they might mean;
but robbers and adulterers,
liars, thieves and murderers
saw meaning in the sands,
as the rocks fell from their hands.

Words etched in proclamation
in the language of three nations
hung up on a cross of wood
above a beaten, bloodied head.
Though truth was clearly scribed
understanding was proscribed;
If you're searching for the proof
these inscriptions speak the truth.

Hologram

I am a living hologram
My light source is unknown
My photon charge is powerful
My visage is full blown
And yet you look right through me
Like a sheet of cellophane
It would be wise to realise
You bring a world of pain

You are a lovely holograph
Your features fine and rare
Your outward beauty captivates
As your photons charge the air
But inside, you're a nightmare
Self-centred, face obsessed
Prosthetics and cosmetics
And, well... you know the rest

Rite

These verses
that I write
as word-smith
and as wright
give voice
to holy rite
that is my
heavenly right

Shudder

I shudder inside when I hear your name
and I shake all over when I see the fame
you attract to yourself at the top of your game
while your entourage tells you who's to blame

I shudder when I wake and I realise
that everything you do is reflected in my eyes
Not a day goes by when my eyes are dry
you make me unhappy but you'll never know why

When I'm in my lonely bed I shudder again
'cos I got your image floating round in my brain
And the thought of you is driving me insane
So I shudder and I shake and I take the pain

But it ain't okay, no it just ain't right
that my life is a misery and yours is so bright
your fame and fortune came without a fight
and I stand in the gutter as I shudder inside

I know life ain't fair but give me a break
at least pay attention to the plea that I make
'cos I shudder inside and you see me shake
it's because of you and me that I'm in this state

Could we get back together, will it ever be?
could you ever stoop down to the level of me?
You are so elevated you're so high and mighty
you forget where you came from originally

You and I are the same, made of the same stuff
You're smooth like silk now, but you once were rough
You came from my 'hood, now you're acting tough
But I know deep inside you're just a powder puff

Girl, how come you and I drifted far apart?
We were star crossed lovers and you held my heart
But you tasted success and you got a new start
and you've turned your aloofness into an art

Don't forget your background, your origin
I can take the hits, I can take it on the chin
But I shudder when I see what we might have been
Now you're up on a pedestal and I'm in the bin

Got one more thing I wanna say to you
Girl, my love for you has always been true
You're rich and famous whatever you do
What I would give for one more rendezvous

But I shudder inside and I shake my head
to think that to you I might as well be dead
Don't get taken in by the lies you were fed
I'm still the best friend that you ever had

Fantasy

I have never fed a unicorn
in a dark enchanted wood
Though I never touched a rainbow,
if I could, you know I would
I have never flown with dragons
'cross the fiery evening skies
and I'll never hold you in my arms
now the fantasy has died

I never swam with mermaids
in the deepest green domain
I have never sailed with pirates
down along the Spanish Main
I have never gathered stardust
in the twinkling of an eye
and I'll never see your loving smile
now the fantasy has died

Pear Shaped

It all began
to go downhill
when God gave
humankind
free will
It soon went
pear shaped,
rapidly,
beneath the boughs
of an apple tree

Counterfeit King

Lies are his key ambition
Deceit is his resting position
Mendacity is his munition
Death is his definition

Life is his consternation
Truth is his contradiction
Light is his putrefaction
Sudden was his eviction

Hell is his benediction
Do you believe his fiction?
He'll fight for your attention
And did I ever mention:

He's a counterfeit king
Wearing ersatz bling
And you'll kiss his ring
If his song you sing

He's an angel of light
A creature of the night
He will blind your sight
When his darkness burns bright

He's the father of lies
Fallen down from the skies
Your eternal soul dies
While your conscience fries

And he'll try to confuse
It's the world's biggest ruse
As you follow his rules
Like all the other fools

Refugees from Paradise

Oh, the tragedy of Eden
all the torment and the pain
to be evicted from the Garden
never to return again

Oh the sadness and the anguish
to be severed from the source
of life and hope and comfort
nothing left but the remorse

To wander in a strange land
refugees from paradise
no home, no hope, no future
victims of our own device

Banished from perfection
from the presence of the One
who cherished us and made us
No more moments in the sun

Oh, the tragedy of Eden
emerging from the rubble
of rebellion in the Garden,
the source of all our trouble

Killer Application

I'm the killer application
inside your imagination
I'm a virtual simulation
I'm the eyes of the whole nation
I'm a sinner and a saint
I'm the slowly drying paint
of graffiti on the wall
I'm the pride before your fall

I'm the earworm in your brain
slowly driving you insane
I'm your sick and dying planet
I'm a mountain made of granite
I'm the one who knows you best
I'm the bullet in your chest
I'm a complicated theory
I'm the sofa when you're weary

I'm your youth and I'm your age
I'm the turning of your page
I'm the inner city violence
I'm the dread inside the silence
I'm the eye of the typhoon
I'm the rains of the monsoon
I'm the next man on the moon
I'm the twenty-first of June

I'm an unknown constellation
I'm your final destination
I'm the vernal equinox
I can open your black box
I'm a raging forest fire
and a dozen false messiahs
I can bring you to your knees
With a mystery disease

I'm relentless on my mission
An indecent proposition
I'm your future and your past
and your clock is running fast
I'm your killer application
I wipe out the competition
Nail your colours to my mast
'Cos it's gonna be a blast

Twisted

Twisted, heavy fisted
broken mirror, pain unlisted
Miasma, flowing magma,
Visions of a glowing plasma

Stalling, fatal falling,
Ugly are the signs of brawling
Growing, never showing
scared eyes see the truth unknowing

Flexion, cold reflection
bruised arms fending in deflection
Violence, vapid silence
ultimately bold defiance

Ever, ending never
Excavating roots to sever
Rising, optimising
Fearfully, the rot excising

Epiphany

The epiphany that came to me
transformed my outlook utterly;
pervaded every part of me;
became my divine odyssey.

What first began as *jamais vu*
was all at once a bird that flew
as I saw what I hitherto
had found elusive, rarely viewed.

My vision came in dead of night
a dream of ethereal insight.
I saw a city, gleaming white
wherein the streets of gold shone bright.

My vision next changed to reveal
a vast meadow of flowering field,
with sparkling streams of life that heal
and fruiting trees of constant yield.

A wondrous pathway next I trod
toward the great White Throne of God
and there I saw with awe and dread
the One from whom all darkness fled.

He had the radiant face of Christ
full iridescent, shining bright.
His mighty throne, the source of light,
made heaven's stratosphere ignite.

A million, million voices sang
worthy is He, the spotless Lamb,
Creator God, the great I Am,
Jesus the King, the Son of Man.

This glorious epiphany
came to my dreams, inspiring me,
for as I glimpsed eternity
I saw through faith my destiny.

One day I'll kneel before His throne
and there I shall cast down my crown.
In radiant robes of white I'll stand,
protected by His nail scarred hands.

Word Up

Word up and word down / the word goes around / and round and around / 'til there ain't no reliable solid ground / and we all look confounded / and astounded / up at the sky and down at the ground / The Word is the only thing that can turn this mess around / we can use words, yeah words, not violence or abuse but words / in the right place and at the right time / whether or not they rhyme / as long as words got rhythm and truth they will get the message out each and every time //

They say actions speak louder than words / but action don't have the power of the verb / the verb, the noun, the adjective / the power is in their collective / 'cos language is more than invective / it's the shot, the bullet, it's the narrative / the words we speak are permanent / laid down in a record that's reverberant / they echo in the mind like a real event / and they pack a punch that's strong like cement. / When your words are sincere and truly meant / they can change your world if it's in your intent //

So I'm dropping my bars like they just been found / and the meaning in the sound / of the words is the crown / and the rhythm in the rhyme grabs you every single time / breaks us out of our confines / gets us needing another line / 'cos nothing else is worth a dime / it removes your bind / opens the eyes of the blind /changes the most stubborn mind / lights up the world like a neon sign / makes our hearts beat in perfect time / and in time / the Word will rhyme / to find the heart / that beats in time / and change the heart / to beat the crime //

Vanity

Mirror on the wall
thy name is vanity
I see your face and
utter a profanity
for you are me in all
my sheer inanity
and narcissism
soon becomes insanity

Monotony Blues

Alarm is sounding
head is pounding
I don't want to
get out of bed
But I must soon
leave my cocoon
I have to meet
the day ahead

Had a skinful
It was sinful
All that alcohol
running through my veins
Now I pay for
what I bayed for
How our lives
drive us insane

Drag myself in
to the bathroom
Avoid the mirror
can't look at me
Try to make me
look unlike me
Fake cosmetic
'surgery'

It's a new day
but I can't say
how thrilled I am
to be me

Sun is shining
but I'm finding
all of this is
monotony

I need something
need a new thing
To remove me
from this rut
How can I fulfil
My potential
open doors that
have been shut

Need to break free
Need a door key
to open up
this prison cage
Need an outlet
from this dragnet
Need a new
performance stage

My head is pounding
The alarm is sounding
I don't want to
leave my bed
But very soon
I leave my cocoon
So I can meet
the day ahead

Overwhelmed

I am overwhelmed
in your presence
when your Spirit
comes to rescue me
It's a mystery
how consistently
my heart dissolves
in ecstasy
I cannot begin to tell you
how you reach
the very core of me

You overwhelm me
with your goodness
You, the spotless
lamb of holiness
my innocent redeemer
my long awaited saviour
You overcome me
with compassion
and there's no question
I am overwhelmed
by your undying passion

The Word

I can't tell you how long I waited
for my freedom, to be liberated.
Now my sin's been obliterated
I'm redeemed, I'm exonerated.

By His love I am dominated
But I've never been indoctrinated
I believe that the truth's been stated
in the Word, it's communicated

In the beginning the Word created
the universe, and He fabricated
everything in six days, unaided
(Please don't ask, 'cos it's complicated)

The Word came and was incarnated,
but His arrival was underrated
He was slated, He was berated
still His love light never faded

While I was still contaminated
I was listening to lies and hatred
For my soul, His blood was traded
From His life He was separated

My redemption was back-dated
to the day that I first got shaded
Now my worth is re-estimated
By His blood I am reinstated

In the Word, it's communicated
that He came and was incarnated
By His blood I am reinstated
I'm redeemed, I am exonerated

He's the Word

Religion is dead

I don't have a religion / and the reasons are legion / it's a schism / it's an imposition / it's a competition / it's a malediction / it causes friction / and constriction /

Religion is a superstition / about ritual and position / it's an inquisition /

[Have faith instead]

Religion / ain't nothing but a condition / a soul incision / a flawed tradition / that causes division / and my decision / is to avoid it with precision / it's my vision / to seek my Creator / this one is on a mission / to serve Him better / follow Him to the letter /

See, my Creator don't want robes / man, that's so intense / He don't need a church or temple / He don't need incense / don't need no wimple / His worship's simple / we become his temple / He lives inside us / feeds the faith in us / grows the grace in us / makes His home in us / and His rule is just / all we need is trust /

Religion / is superstition / about ritual and position / it's an inquisition /

[Have faith instead]

He don't need rose petals / no golden vessels / no holy medals /

He don't ask for shekels / He's no man's debtor / and it gets
even better / there's none that is greater / than our Creator /
don't need a religion / to commune with your maker / He's a
life giver / not a life taker / He's the genuine thing / He ain't
no faker /

Religion is superstition / about ritual and position /
it's an inquisition / it's a contradiction /

[Have faith instead]

Take faith instead / get it in your head / He ain't on that
crucifix / He ain't dead / man, He ain't even sick / 'cos the
angels said:

"Why you looking for the living / among the dead? / He rose
just like He said." / He ain't on no death-bed / so take faith
instead / get it into your head / religion is dead /

[Have faith instead]

Fathom

Around, over and under
floating distant sounds of thunder
livid through consciousness
cold blows the wind
from out the west
all but devised
I see the
look gleam
in your eyes
and wonder
what the mind
behind
has found
and whether its discovery
may be profound
I cannot fathom out
the thoughts of doubt
you hold within your
stone shield redoubt
the bulwarks of
your soul
impenetrable
as the ancient
living
rock

.

.

.

.

When Salvation comes to Town

Society will be revised
the revolution will be televised
the changes shown before our eyes
not sanitised, no compromise

The violent struggles of the past
will be no more, they will not last
The people will repent *en masse*
when our salvation comes to pass

Hypocrisy will be unwound
and tyranny will not be found
for truth and justice will be crowned
when peace our citadel surrounds

We'll take our weapons, melt them down
bury our failures in the ground
uphold the good, raise up the sound
when our salvation comes to town

Great White Throne

Plastic surgeons, foolish virgins
Diamond merchants, back street urchins
Broadcasters, smoking Rastas
Old masters, evangelical pastors
Document printers, Olympic sprinters
Eligible spinsters, confidence tricksters
Civil engineers, little old dears
Pioneers and racketeers
Bombardiers and brigadiers
Auctioneers and volunteers
Puppeteers and mutineers
He/him and she/her
They/them and every other gender
Biologists, psychologists
Biochemists and physicists
Mathematicians, geriatricians
Neonatal paediatricians
Lorry drivers, deep sea divers
Faith healers, used car dealers,
Bouncers, exotic dancers
Scroungers and loungers
Librarians, libertarians, contrarians
Rock musicians, electricians
Au pairs, millionaires
Restauranteurs and connoisseurs
Kings and queens, college deans
Captains of nuclear submarines
Magnificent men in their flying machines
Dreamers of impossible dreams
Methodists and pacifists

Buddhists and masochists,
Sadists and narcissists
Those that hit and those that miss
Followers of Islam and followers of Shiva
The quietest voices and the loudest diva
Presbyterians, veterinarians
Vegetarians and pescatarians
Benedictine monks, muscle bound hunks
Hopeless drunks, rebellious punks
Toreadors and matadors,
Ambassadors and red-light whores
Astrologer, police officer
Philosopher, photographer
Angel and demon,
Bond man and free man
He-man, she-man
and every other hu-man
At the end of time
when all is said and done
all of us will bow before
the Great White Throne

Run

Let your feet pound the pavement
Run as swiftly as you can
May your legs stride out in freedom
on the earth and through the sand

Let the breezes swirl around you
down these avenues of stone
Run strong and keep on running
You will never run alone

Run the distance, faithful athlete
stretch each sinew and each limb
though tiredness may slow you
and your vision may grow dim

Throw off your heavy burdens
so your running may be light
through the good times and the bad times
as you press on through the night

Keep your eyes upon the prize
and your focus on your goal
to complete your race with honour
by the courage of your soul

Reflected in your Eyes

Reflected in your eyes I see
four hundred years of misery
the memories of iron chains,
of lives spent in captivity

Reflected in your eyes I see
the pain and the fear of
endless famine and brutality

Reflected in your eyes I see
the injustice and the prejudice
of those so blind they will not see

Reflected in your eyes I see
the memories of your family
torn open, never more to be free

Reflected in your eyes I see
a deep yearning for freedom
and the noble fight for equity

Reflected in your eyes
I see a hope for future liberty
for a world set free from misery
released from inhumanity
a world set free

NRG

Our energy
comes from
you and me
from our ecstasy
and our jealousy

Clever

Clever with rhymes
clever with phrases
not so good at
remembering faces
Clever with words
clever with verses
poor at emotional
reverses

The World, Reset

The world hung in a blue screen
suspended functionality
Keyboard dead, flashing red
no hope, no possibility
A planet silent running
no connection was detected
This world a broken terminal
its software was infected
Then came the major reset
The manufacturer appeared
The world was placed in quarantine
all hardware re-engineered
He died and then was buried
and the planet was shut down
When He rose up from the grave
the Earth rebooted once again
'cos He dealt with the virus
that had invaded our system
He deleted the infection
that was holding us to ransom
He emptied out this planet
of the things beyond our control
and offered us the vaccine
to the virus in our souls
There's now a simpler algorithm
to improve our spiritual health:
Love God with all your strength and soul
and your neighbour as yourself

Paid on the Nail

You can try to silence me but
I'm still gonna praise Him
you can try to shut me down
but I'm still gonna raise Him
you can put me in the corner,
you won't stop me saying His name
you can side-line me, but
you can't take me out of the game
you can take away my freedom,
but I get to keep my faith
you can throw away the key,
I'm a still gonna walk free
'cos He ain't gonna let nobody
lay their hands on me
you can keep me in the darkness,
I'm a still see His light
I can see Him in His glory
though you take away my sight
ain't nowhere you can put me
I can't see Him on His throne
ain't nowhere you can isolate me
'cos I'll never be alone
You can beat me try to break me
I ain't never giving in
you can leave me and forsake me
but He took away my sin
whatever I'm in, He'll see me through
He'll never let me down
He will even raise me up
when I'm a six feet underground
in sickness or in health

in riches or in despair
He's the only one my mind's fixed on
'cos He's the only one who cares
You can hate me
you can doubt me
but you'll never grind me down
you can call me names,
drop me the blame,
I ain't never turning round
try anything you like to
ridicule who you think I am
but the truth is you can't separate
me from the Great I Am
There ain't a thing in this world
that can deviate my path
You see, one plus one is four,
but you can never do the math
He is the three in one,
and I'm the apple of His eye
He's the Ancient of Days,
and He will never ever die
I am bought with a price,
I am paid for on the nail
and I'm standing on His promises,
'cos they will never, ever fail.

Jump Scare

My life
is one big
jump scare
after another
jump scare
Jump ..
SCARE!

oh mother
It's another
jump scare
I never saw
that one
coming

You'll see me with
a rictus grin
I'm not enjoying
this scene I'm in
I'm pulling off
a calm impression
but underneath
there's a soul
compression
and I'm
jumping inside

In the placid pools
of peace
I can no longer paddle
I have ceased

they are polluted
and diseased
by toxins of terror
they are demented
by the detritus
of error
Defeated by deeds
of desperation
Scarred by the scares
Jump scares

rapidly repeating
moments of miasma
and madness
Roll across me
on my pathway
leaping out
to scare me
Jump ...
SCARE!

You'll see me with
a rictus grin
I'm not enjoying
this scene I'm in
I'm pulling off
a calm impression
but underneath
there's a soul
compression

and I'm
jumping inside ….

Insipid hours
are rudely interrupted
by unexpected episodes
of agony and angst
waiting for
the next
jump ….

SCARE!!

Languid days
lacerated by
The ice cold
fingernails of fear
scraping at
the thin veneer

Jump scares
just around
the corner
everywhere

Did he jump
or was he scared?

Einstein Dreams

Just like those
suspect quotes
ascribed to
Albert Einstein,
nothing is quite
what it seems
but is fabricated
fabulously

Like the times
when I
still see you
in my dreams

The Torn Veil

Hidden, in the temple,
set apart, a holy place
The world could not transgress
the boundaries of this sacred space
Once only in each passing year,
in reverence and in fear
a priest within the holy place
would timidly appear

The veil a boundary between
a fallen world and holiest place
where only priests could hope to
meet with the Ancient of Days
It symbolised a gulf that
divides men from God above
one that could only be bridged
by a great sacrifice of love

Then came the day the Nazarene
in lowly clothes appeared
A builder's son with callused hands
and eyes of fire that seared
into the very heart and soul
with love's amazing grace
And finally, men spoke with
their Creator face to face

Though many could not see it,
a light in the darkness shone,
His heart screamed out eternal love,

but the people's choice was wrong
The Lamb of God rejected,
died between the earth and sky
and three days hidden in a tomb,
for He was born to die

At His final breath,
the veil tore as if to say:
The gulf between us,
God and man,
has now been torn away
Now enter in with no more fear,
whoever will may come
into the holiest place,
for it is finished, it is done

This Man

Who was he, this man from Nazareth?
This outcast Jew, this sunburnt warrior?
A soldier with no iron,
who held no weapon of war
who fought and won a decisive battle
on a dark Judean hill?
A pacifist who turned the tables over,
a placid man who screamed his anger
in the temple while the cheating
money changers fled?
A sorcerer that angry waves obeyed
who commanded the violent winds to cease?
A lunatic the common people
loved and followed?
A zealot feared and hated
by the religious high command?

Who was he, this man of Galilee,
this wandering man in plainest clothes
who spoke with prostitutes and kings
who owned no home or property?
A narcissist who claimed to be the
gateway into everlasting life?
The human face of the Creator God?
A poet who spoke peace
and life in prose,
and metaphors that
few could understand?
A liar who made claims and promises
so outrageous that many still cannot believe?

Who was he, this outcast
renegade of the Roman state?
A conjuror who magicked bread and fish,
who walked on water and through walls?
A physician who revived the dead,
restored sight to the blind
and healed the sick?
An illusionist who
finessed the finest wine
from water in a common village well?
A patriot who shouted his sedition
against a dark, oppressive occupying force?
An idealist who opposed hypocrisy
and corruption in the corridors of power?

Who was he, this man of deepest mystery?
Who disappeared for days on end
in desert wasteland,
who reappeared transformed?
Was he a superhero or a villain,
a mutant or an alien,
or just a humble Hebrew carpenter?

Were there splinters in his hands,
hands that healed,
the hands fixed down by the nails?
Were there shavings in his hair,
hair that was torn out,
hair adorned by cruel thorns?

Was there deceit inside his mouth,
the mouth that uttered love

the mouth that spoke forgiveness?
Was there honesty behind those eyes,
eyes that saw the future,
eyes that closed in death?
Was there any life inside that corpse,
his broken body laid to rest
inside that borrowed tomb?

Did he fulfil his promise,
or was his body stolen by timid friends
who overpowered a force of Roman guards?
The same who feared and ran away to hide?
Did he roll the heavy stone aside
and fold his burial garments there?
Was he seen again, walking, talking
eating, sitting down along the lakeside shore?
Did he show the nail prints in his hands?
The spear wound in his side?
Was he who he claimed to be?
What will you decide?

Who was this man?

I Will Stand

All that is of value
the pure gold
from the mould
All the eternal riches
I can hold
that unfold
in each dream of hope
that takes flight
in its might
Every deep desire
shining bright
in deepest night
All are found in you
by the plans
from your hands
Underneath your wings
I will stand
I will stand

Storms

Staring down into the black abyss
We should all be terrified at this
Our hearts should quiver and our bodies quake
but my fears are asleep, while my soul awakes

Gazing out unto the bleak unknown
As kings and kingdoms are overthrown
Our works are broken and our words undone
There is nothing new underneath the sun

If I could search the entire realms of man
Still I would never really understand
why it was to me you held out your hand
How there came to be two sets of
footprints in the sand

Now I'm unafraid and my faith won't shade it
'Cos, I stand on the Rock and you can't degrade it
The storms of circumstance can't shake it
'Cos I have His promise and I know I'll make it
When the world crashed no-one else could save it
I wouldn't wanna stand alone to brave it
Safe in His arms when the tidal wave hit
Yeah, I hold the hand of the One who made it

A Last Hail Mary

The world we humans occupy
this world in which we are contained
has walls of matter, boundaries of sky
and curtains made from falling rain

How often do we try to breach
those naturally occurring walls
to grasp for things beyond our reach
as mystery and forbidden knowledge calls?

The greatest barrier of time
is found in heartbeats of the great and small
given to a natural rhyme
measured by the rhythm, rise and fall

The world we inhabit is strange and contrary
and can rapidly descend into scary
a place of turmoil where we
seek to say the prayer we
all learnt at the last hail Mary

Golden Light

Within the empires of my mind
and through all my great imaginings;
across the vast, empty terrains of time
and in the folly of my frantic gatherings;
within the chambers of my heart
or flashing 'cross the unseen universe,
my life and soul ends where it starts,
I live for better or for worse.

None could replace the music of your voice
the frisson of your smiling face,
and no amount of warm solace
could substitute for your amazing grace.
So in my lucid waking dreams
I hold onto your presence tight
the emptiness of loss, I fear
and the dying of your fragile, golden light.

Rock Paper Scissors

The fist
that missed
a hundred times or more
to make
or break;
the fist that raps
upon your door

Unless
the rest
can flatten out this tortuous curve,
the odds
are even
that they will never
hold their nerve

But I,
like you,
am in a hypervigilant state
and you,
like me,
will cut the tie that
causes us to hate

Life Lines

Life with you was never breezy,
left me feeling so uneasy,
feeling stupid never clever,
no convergence prospects ever,
like the tram lines

Lovers strolling in the woods,
doing just what young love should
Holding hands and passing time,
inextricably entwined
in heart lines

Their relationship was rocky,
never saw it as unlucky,
but then it all went to the wall
and when bad luck came round to call,
it was hard lines

Breakdown in communication
caused us lots of consternation,
outward nodding, inner leaning,
misunderstandings, double meaning,
in those crossed lines

Famous for all the wrong reasons,
in the fast lane for a season,
before it all came crashing down
so suddenly the day they found
you in the headlines

Saw you standing at the bar,
wishing on a fallen star,
like to get to know you more,
quickly searching through my store
of pickup lines

Waiting in intensive care,
holding back the grief you bear,
nothing more that you can say,
life signs slowly ebb away
to a flatline

Been away for many years,
travelling through a veil of tears,
home to loved ones, friends you missed,
remembering the boy you kissed
near the railway line

Suicidal, dark thoughts reign,
when the black dog growls its name
In the night you fear you'll fall,
seeking help you choose to call
the night line

Single minded, on a mission,
never need to ask permission.
Knows just what she wants from life,
butter cut with a hot knife
She takes a bee line

Got no money got no stash,
envious of those with cash
Rob and steal to stay alive,
barely able to survive
on the bread line

Running hard to beat the clock,
ticking seconds, never stop
When the hours and minutes fly,
you make sure you keep your eye
on the deadline

Balancing on the high wire,
one misstep I'm in the fire,
fear is my constant company,
vertigo my enemy
I walk a fine line

She's the prodigal daughter
who was dead in the water
Going down for the final time,
a tragedy in her own maritime
Throw her a life line

Quicksand

One day, inevitably, I will
flounder in a quicksand
of my own design. One day –
and that day is coming –
I must moulder in the morass
of my own making. And as
I am fighting uselessly to
resist that fatal undertow,
I will remember the good times
and the bad, and I will think of you.
I will hold on to the one thing
left within my flailing grasp. I will
rue the times we never had,
and I will regret the ruination
of the tenderness, the demise
of the affection, the slow falling
of our fortunes. It is coming.
One day, inevitably, I will
flounder in the quicksand
of my own design.

Dependence Day

You beg for mercy in the midday sun
You look for peace in the shadow of the gun
You run from trouble when it's just begun
so hide beneath the wings of the Risen One
Okay, I'm gonna take this to church
I ain't gonna leave you in the lurch
not gonna knock you off your perch
just gonna give you cause to search
'Cos when you seek then you will find
push on the door, see what's behind
He'll give you freedom when you're in a bind
He restores sight to those who are blind
He has the keys to the prison door
When you plead for justice, He'll settle the score
with abundant grace you cannot ignore
(you ask for three and He'll give you four)
He's gonna take you wherever He'll lead
He got the power and He got the speed
The wealth you crave is just chicken feed
when He owns everything you'll ever need
So don't run and hide from the truth, the way
His blood will wash all your sins away
Don't wish for an independence day
You can lean on Him, He'll be your mainstay

Lies

there is
  contradiction
      in your diction
  there's a friction
    in your fiction
        and the lies
      in your eyes
    compromise
      your disguise
        your capacity
          for mendacity
            and duplicity
              has frequency
        you conceal
and double deal
    your surreal
    lies congeal
sowing seeds
    of misdeeds
      you mislead
      guaranteed

More than meets the Eye

There is a lot more to see
beyond your visual acuity
There is much more to this
than you believe exists.
If you use other eyes
you will begin to realise
our material world is lies
an enigma in disguise.
There is much more to this
than a hug and a kiss.
Love is more than physical
love is wholly mystical
the mystery and the wonder
of the lightning and thunder
goes deeper, takes you under
gives you chills, breaks you asunder.
If you look beyond the visions
of your earthly contradictions
and you search inside your soul
see the parts that make the whole
then you'll see a fuller meaning
to the life that you are leading

Your Name

I only need to hear your name
to feel those shivers down my spine.
I only have to see your face
to know of ecstasy divine.

There is a nuance in your name
that causes me to contemplate
how I could ever live without
your awesome power to elevate.

Heaven's Gateway

The gateway into heaven is not forged from gold or pearls;
It's a trans-dimensional portal into another world.
Transition from this finite time into that eternal realm
is a sudden, one-way journey from which there's no return.

Transition is instantaneous; there's no time to acclimatise
as you watch your world transforming before your open eyes
to colours unimaginable, beyond earthly comprehension,
and time will cease to flow, inside that eternal dimension.

The laws of science and man will one day fade into oblivion,
as souls fly to their destination in the beautiful Elysium.
There, standing at the centre, above a sea of glass,
is the throne room of the Ancient One, the future and the past

The Ancient of all Days, the Almighty God of old
who reigns in glorious power in that City made of gold.
Though anyone may enter, if they love the Risen One
the gateway into heaven cannot welcome everyone.

Outside the walls are those who gamble with a loaded dice.
The Redeemed are those whose trust lay in His final sacrifice.
The Lamb of God will separate pure sheep from goats of sin
on that final reckoning day, when the souls are gathered in.

Own Goal

I pushed you away when
I should have held you close
I turned my back on you
when you needed me the most

My choices have wounded
our lonely fragile souls
Too many unforced errors
too many own goals

Have you seen the Moon?

Have you seen the moon?
Have you really looked?
A harsh mistress or a dainty maid
A balloon deflated and then remade
By day or night in light or in shade
A pockmarked elusive renegade
Have you seen the moon?
Have you really looked?

Have you seen the stars?
Have you really looked?
A string of iridescent beads
A shiny scattering of seeds
A glowing carpet on the breeze
and all the wonder that it breeds
Have you seen the stars?
Have you really looked?

Dig Deep

Dig deep
Excavate
Search out
and navigate
What is the
Meaning of
your life?

Think through
Contemplate
Find out
and Illuminate
What is the
Meaning of
Your life?

Knock loud
Resonate
Push hard
Don't hesitate
Find out the
Meaning of
your life

Advocate

Everything I've ever done
Laid down in ink, eternal re-run
Everything I've ever said
Recorded from my life's first breath
Everything I've ever thought
Stored up in everlasting vaults
Each outburst, every curse I've thrown
Preserved for ever, carved in stone
Secrets kept, never disclosed
Transfixed in brightness and exposed

Ashamed I kneel before the Throne
My spirit stained, alone, alone
But then appears my advocate
Him, my eternal surrogate
Who died for me to take my place
To grant my soul amazing grace
Who paid that dreadful purchase price
At Calvary's brutal sacrifice
I now stand blameless, this I know
Cleansed fully by His crimson flow

Dreaming

Sleep falls slowly
like a summer dew
so surreptitiously
upon my brow.
My dreams arise
like mermaid sighs
then just as freely
they recede like tides.
Somnambulant,
I tread the paths
of steaming gardens
long ago oppressed
by topic heat
that drips from leaves
and flows to ground
beneath my feet.
And in my dreams
there's not a sound;
the colours fade
to grey within
imagined space.
For in my dreams
I cannot see your face.

Look for Me

You will hear me in the thunder
rolling loudly 'cross the skies
You will see me in the lightning
and the power it supplies
You will sense me in the calmness
of a balmy afternoon
and discern me in the shining
of the full faced harvest moon
You will sense me in the numbers
of the planets as they flow
and perceive me in the stillness
of the freshly fallen snow
You will know me in the faces
of your children as they play
and you'll find me in the sunset
at the ending of your day

This Old Dog

Easy son, your time will come
You'll have your moment in the sun
So turn around without a sound
and plant your feet firm to the ground

Right now (and here I coin a phrase)
This body has seen better days
But don't be fooled by ageing looks
The cover does not define the book

I know you're standing in the wings
Like princes do before they're kings
But son, your time has not yet come
These feet still have more miles to run

One day you'll step into the breech
To exercise your length of reach
Until that day, let no one ever say
That this old dog has had his day

Human

For all,
we are human
and our choices
are plain

Some seek ecstasy
and others pain

Acrostic Instruments

My earliest memories
Under cloudless blue skies
Singing wondrous rhapsodies
Immersed in melodic harmonies
Conducting my glorious symphonies.

Instruments of every shape and
Size, their mellow sounds still have

The power to hypnotise. And more, to
Hold the source of such surprise,
Empowers my soul to extemporise.

For music has the power, the poise, to
Overwhelm, to bring me joy no
Other sound, no other noise could ever
Demonstrate or so employ.

Oh, music, I would be so lost if
For any reason, or from any cost you

Left my side and disappeared into some
Other place, where I could not access the
Very essence of your grace. I would be for
Ever lost without your inspiration.

Wrong Turn

You should be singing hymns
instead, you're hanging with the crims.
You wear snapbacks, and your bling
is shocking. Where'd you get that thing?

Making trouble in the neighbourhood,
you ain't living like you know you should.
You ain't never gonna make the grade
while you're throwing all that shade.

You took some wrong turns, and you're lost
but somebody already paid the cost
to set you free from your double dealing.
Get on your knees, and receive some healing.

The Road Less Taken

Now here's a thought you can incubate / what happens when you eventually get into a state / where you realise that things are not quite as great / as they say they are? Do you wait / and do you hesitate / or do you crash on through like it's much too late?

How do you throw it / when your garden don't grow it / and you're hurting and you know it / but you got no room to show it / and your family and friends don't know it / and you're carrying the weight on your own / reaping the whirlwind you have sown / catching the hardball that's been thrown / feeling your heartache to the bone / when you're vulnerable and you're prone / to a fear of the unknown / standing there in the darkness all alone?

How do you cut it when you're hated / and berated / and your words are denigrated / or you're blamed for a crime someone else perpetrated / falsely accused or underrated / misunderstood and understated / cleaning up the mess someone else created / undervalued, ignored and slated / your character assassinated?

When you know a date / with hate / is not the way to perambulate / how do you deviate? / When you know it's not your fate / to return the hate / and to retaliate / do you stop and contemplate? / An eye for an eye and a tooth for a tooth / the world cries out from the top of the roofs / ain't that the truth / but it's not the road to ride and I'll show you the proof

All the people in this world are on a stage / we're all reading
our script from the same old page / living in the age / of the
rage / where we're all locked up in the same cage / living the
outrage

….and there are entrances and exits for all the players / but
everyone got their layers / and we all want out but we can't
see where the way is / and they exit is not where they say it is
/ and we're running in circles as we tear / out our hair / it's
more than most of us can bear / to be at peace with life is rare
/ but if you dig deeper through the layers / and you say a
little prayer / to the higher power / the One who really do
care / then you'll find your way out man, it's there / right in
front of you, right there / standing beyond the public glare

it's the gate that's narrow and the road less taken / so look for
it and find it, and feel your soul reawaken /

Minus Thirty-Three Degrees

The echelons of absolute power
have their roots in brotherhood
and closely guarded secrets,
'cos they're never up to any good

Designated parking spaces
for the designated ruling class
The rich men and the bankers
use the wealth they have amassed

They trade in funny handshakes,
make decisions 'on the nod'
They speak of a great architect
but they don't refer to God

They live their lives of luxury,
they never have a care
Portrayed as all round good guys,
they are always on the square

They'd get away with murder
'cos the judge is one of them
Their misdemeanours covered up
by influential men

Their aprons and their blindfolds
seem a lot like fun and games
But their goals are deadly serious
and lives are in the frame

Their deeds are done in darkness
and are speculative at least
But it really doesn't matter
while they're Sitting in the East

Their lodges wouldn't welcome
the likes of you and I
Closing up their ranks to shield
their craft from prying eyes

They use respectability
as a cloak to hide their crime
They'll go to any lengths
to cover what their lives enshrine

It's time to leave them in the cold,
to put them in deep freeze
Let's turn the thermostat
to minus thirty-three degrees

Faded

Forlorn was I, and faded,
bleached out beneath
an unforgiving sun.
My soul torn and jaded
in unbelief, I fell just
as my journey had begun.

In darkness I was stumbling,
a stain on my behaviour,
no map to show my way;
not a light to guide my rambling.
But then I met the Saviour,
heard what He had to say.

He told me truths
that cut through me like
the coldest stormy day
and all the blues I used to play
are now washed out,
they are faded away.

Mark of Cain

Hatred never wins;
it will not stand,
it won't sustain.

The fear of difference,
and of others
is the mark of Cain.

In simple incredulity
we sit here
and we contemplate
just how small minded
and ignorant
are the fools
who practise hate

Machinery of the Darkness

The machinery of the darkness
shapes the rhythms of the day;
car headlights trace our walls
inscribing words we wish to say;
the wounded of the night fall
down the stairwells of alarm,
and we are found in doorways
with our pockets full of harm

> The gears grind
> and the engines roar,
> and calm is drowned alive,
> but still we swarm together
> like the bees within a hive

Did you once promise me
that all my honesty would pay?
Was there once a perfect time
and place when you would pray
to golden deities, and ancient
chariots of the gods?
When all is evened out
why do we find ourselves at odds?

The gears grind
and the engines roar,
and calm is drowned alive,
while rebels and delinquents pause
to sharpen up their knives

Where our two lives diverged
there is a fracture in the rocks;
while you are charmed by witches
and the ticking of the clocks,
and I am sore distracted by
the squalor that I see,
the machinery of the darkness
growls in shadows threateningly

The gears grind
and the engines roar,
and calm is drowned alive,
but we assemble in our fears
just trying to survive

Remind Me

Remind me, when
did we last meet?
You're not so quick
upon your feet,
The clock ticks on
the years accrete
Your tempo slowed
to a different beat

When was the last time
that we spoke?
When we were young
we went for broke
and not a thing
could fear invoke
Life was for fun,
and one big joke

Now we are older
and replete
we spend our days
in comfy seats
and we're less steady
on our feet ...

Remind me, when
did we last meet?

Fighter

Down but never out, although
I'm floored, I'm undefeated
I get back up again because
I'm tired but not depleted
Always in with a chance each time
I fight with the conceited
They'll never be expecting
that this *soufflé* is reheated

I got my second wind and my
manoeuvres just got lighter
My foes will fear my aim because
they know I'm a straight sighter
I'll go the distance every time
'cos I'm an undefeated fighter
I serve the One who formed the stars
He couldn't be more mightier

So do your worst and throw that punch
I'll hit back twice as hard
You'll soon be wishing you were
safe at home in your back yard
Each round I'll come right back at you
and I'll catch you off your guard
You'll be face down on the canvas
when you get my calling card

Gardening Leave

They partied hard, up to the hilt
inside the garden that they built
but left it eaten up with guilt
and that's the old, old story

The fruit with bite marks evidence
that they had lost their common sense
and perpetrated their offence
Their error, *a priori*

What was idyllic got destroyed
'cos girls were girls, and boys were boys
They took what wasn't theirs – bad choice
it turned into their folly

They really got their fingers burnt
and there's a lesson to be learnt
First they were, and then they weren't
They did it for some glory

Love life and live it to the max
but don't forget the cold, hard facts
you have your fun, then pay the tax
and it's the same sad story

You pays your money, drinks your beer
but it'll all end up in tears
if your actions make you disappear
from the eternal inventory

Battle

Every time I transgress / and I'm battling this stress / a small part of my soul dies in distress / each time I'm caught up in this stress / I have to confess / my life feels like a total mess / I feel repressed / and depressed / and oppressed / and I try to suppress / and yeah, right, you guessed / everything I possess / is about to be repossessed / but the reepo says there ain't nothing of value to repossess / and he's not impressed / and that's the story of my life, I guess //

Each one of my sick feats and blunders / remind me one day I'll be six feet and under / but in the meantime my life is being torn asunder / just as under / a roll of thunder / so it's no wonder / for the third time I feel like I'm going under / but I'm a remind myself this is a battle I'm in and I won't surrender //

In every single line I'm writing / you can see I'm a keep on fighting / though it keeps on biting / I'm a stand under the hot spotlighting / become totally visible under the light in / the centre, standing there in the room I'm in / in the place I've been given / I ain't gonna turn tail and take flight, I'm / a totally stand and fight / the frightening / take it on / full headlong / and keep it strong / even though the battle may be long / cos this kinda stuff is totally wrong / and it don't belong / in my mind or in my life or in my song //

Cold day in Hell

Get thee behind me Satan,
there's a queue
There's more to life than
listening to the likes of you
So crawl back in your hole
like you know you should
There never was a time when
you were up to any good

Your days are numbered
and it won't be very long
Before you face the music
and sing your final song
Your audience will jeer as
you listen to them boo
It'll be a cold day in Hell
before I pay attention to you

Foreign Skies

....under foreign skies
we all wander,
our eyes wide, gazing
searching for landmarks
amid unfamiliar places
trying to remember

....we are all foreigners
in this distant land
far from our birthplaces,
disconnected from our times,
severed from our country

....our belongings are scattered
across our histories
strewn in the highways
of our memories and
hanging, caught among
the briar thorns of our regrets

....how many times
my father
wandered aimlessly
searching for familiar places
he remembered,
while the world
around him changed

Young Warriors

I sent them out,
my young warriors,
into the field of conflict;
into harm's way –
but not before they
were ready to do battle.
I trained them well,
those young warriors;
I trained them to discern
the difference between
the truth and a lie
and to defend themselves
against attack from all sides;
I trained them to assault
and defeat the wrongs
society has perpetuated
and perpetrated.
I sent them out,
those young fighters,
into a world of indifference;
to break down structures
of imprisonment and harm;
to build new worlds
where children can be free
to run, explore and create;
to think for themselves.

I sent them out,
these young warriors,
to wage a war of words,
to bring justice
and understanding.
I sent them forth,
my quiet commandos,
my *guerrillas liberales*.
Some have since fallen
others wounded in the fray
but they have made
the difference,
my young warriors,
in every way.

Past Perfect Tense

This ain't no strange coincidence
and I can say this with confidence
that we all just lost our innocence
deep in the silence
of this age of violence
and maybe you just lost your common sense
if all you want is some recompense
some retribution for some vile offense
that sits in your head like a present tense
like an enemy air defence
or like an image of Mike Pence

Now the future's super tense
well it is, in a past participle sense
with our citizens all living in suspense
because our politicians
are still sat on the fence
and we live through this political pretence
but the fence has just been painted
and now they've all been tainted
but they ain't repenting
and they ain't relenting
and they ain't gonna be consenting
to a change in their direction

If you want real change
(and if you don't you're pretty strange)
then you have to rearrange
the status quo from outside of the outrage
not from the audience but from on the stage
there ain't no sense heckling

and barracking from the back of the room
ain't no use calling in remote by Zoom
you might as well be talking
from the inside of a tomb

You gotta be there at the front
with the microphone
you need to be present in the zone
you need to hone
an authoritative tone
that channels your people's groans
and moans
and make no bones
for justice to be done
and I tell you this brother, sister –
you ain't alone
so stand up
and take that microphone

Battle Cry

Clandestine,
slipping undetected
into an alien dimension
under the radar, his identity
disguised and scarcely mentioned
except in allegories and metaphors
with a divine precision
heavily armed with nothing
but love, and on a sacred mission
to release the hostages
that the enemy had taken

He was wounded outside walls
of a foreign town, forsaken
by his own people while
exchanging fire inside the kill zone
plunged into absolute darkness
dying, and all alone
while battling valiantly
with his ancient adversary
in an occupied
Middle Eastern territory

Though it looked like
a forlorn and hopeless mess
his mission was
an unequivocal success
the secret warrior died
but was far from finished
and in his death his strength
was not diminished

when this heroic soldier
met his warrior death
and his comrades watched
him draw his final breath
they gently laid him
deep inside the ground
and they thought they heard
the demons dance around
as his unmarked grave
fell into screaming silence
like a footnote to demark
this act of violence
but consistent with
his own prophetic words
something deep inside
that dark tomb stirred ...

Two mornings later
as the sun was rising
his comrades locked down
inside their homes and hiding
with their ravaged hearts
exposed to dark despair
their courage dissipating
into the air
the warrior burst out
just like a lion roaring
and sent his comrades'
sunken spirits soaring

He showed them
his battle wounds
and in his victory
over death, deep inside
the enemy's territory
his love would now
become their battle cry
their theatre of war
the souls of you and I

Let's Get Lost Together

Let's get lost together
down the back streets
of a foreign city
Let's lose our way
in winding lanes
that lead us nowhere
Let's find ourselves
in lonely fields of wheat
swept by the raucous wind
Let's wander aimlessly
across uncharted territory
Let no map save us
Let's walk the unfamiliar ground
toward a mutual oblivion
Let's stroll together
into a strange wilderness
and never find our way
back home again

Nailed

You can nail a shingle to your office wall
Screw a photo frame secure so it won't fall
You can nail a horseshoe up above your door
Nail a hundred objects high, or even more

You can pin your pictures to an album page
or secure a backdrop to a drama stage
You can fasten any object as you will
but Christ climbed willingly up that hill

The nails did not secure Him to that tree
The spikes did not prevent Him being free
but love became His sole constraint
and Christ died for the sinner, not the saint

Divergence

The divergence of our history
and memories of the mystery
surround our glorious past
Alas, like rain it didn't last

The cadence of our union
then the sudden separation
Oh, the turbulence of touch
It didn't hurt that much

The division bell was sounded
and our parting was compounded
Since we went our separate ways
I have seen far better days

All Too Soon

Leaden skies and a harvest moon
say summer ended all too soon.
The autumn leaves hang on like prayers
changed to the colours of your hair.

and we are lonely souls inside
with yearning yet unsatisfied.
Our hearts search for an August sun
but autumn has already come.

As evening falls, a glittering star
blinks into sight, but wanders far
through cloud with golden lining hidden
obscuring skies as yet unwritten.

and still we cling to age old fears
as we gaze back on yesteryears,
and leaden skies, and harvest moons.
Our summer ended all too soon.

Beyond the White Veil

I speak with the tongues
of both angels and man
I write with full tempo
in verses that scan
I speak of the wonders
beyond the white veil
I point to the splendours
that were paid on the nail
I can only imagine
what waits for us there
and I fail to do justice
in verse or in prayer
I write in a language
inadequate, poor
that cannot describe
that fair otherworld shore
I write of the Meadow
and the streams that will heal
I picture the Throne Room
where His presence is real
and I know deep inside
without words to pursue
there's a mansion made ready
for the faithful and true
Yes, I know in my heart
without vocabulary
that He's preparing a place
that's especially for me

Yardstick

You can measure life with coffee spoons
or measure it in miles
You can measure life in miracles
or measure it in smiles
You can measure life in cellophane,
and try to wrap the stars
You can mark your time with consequence
or measure life in hours

You can mark it with relationships
and measure it with friends
or choose the road of solitude
with trials that never end
You can measure life with fingers
and count every digit span
or choose the path of violence
and hold weapons in your plan

You can choose a life of peacefulness
and measure it in healing
or a life of disbelief where
your prayers bounce off the ceiling
You can measure out your days in fear
where all things are a threat
or live a life of trust, where
every day your life's reset

You can measure life materially
in money and possessions
by how much wealth you can amass
with your mercantile obsessions

Your life's weighed in the balance
and what will tip the scale?
Will it be your great successes
or your string of hopeless fails
or the cash you gave to charity,
all the money you have raised?
Do you think they'll serve to save you,
or that God will be amazed?

No matter what your yardstick,
time is running out for you
and time stands still for no-one
it's a door we all walk through
'cos the journey that you started
on is the journey you will end
and the measure of your life will be
if you can call Him 'friend'

Nine Million

I write my blog, nine million people read it
I walk my dog, but anyone could lead it
I have a habit, and other people feed it
and it's only me that can concede it

I write a book and all the hacks review it
I tie my shoelace, you try to undo it
Nine million people wish for other faces
and I desire to be nine million other places

Walk with Me

Walk with me when your friends turn back
Walk with me when the skies turn black
When the wild dogs bark, and the mad crowds yell
and your life feels just like an empty shell
When you're standing outside the gates of Hell
In the midst of an enemy sneak attack
Walk with me

Walk with me when you feel the strain
and your world is drowned in a sea of pain
When the lonely night makes you cry out loud
and you're lost in the throng of a faceless crowd
When there's no escape from the thunder cloud
and you're soaked to the skin in the pouring rain
Walk with me

Walk with me when you're in distress
Walk with me when your life's a mess
When you see no future and there's no way out
and your mind is filled with the darkest doubt
and all you want is to scream and shout
Though the worst may happen, nonetheless
Walk with me

Prodigal Child

Forgive me Father, I failed to see
the harm I caused so recklessly
I failed to see the full extent
of the selfishness in my intent

I do the things I shouldn't do
which drives a wedge 'tween me and you
I don't do all the things I should
I'm rarely up to any good

Bear with me Lord although this hype'll
show I'm not your best disciple
My spirit's strong but my will is weak
I'm playing heavenly hide and seek

I'm a prodigal child and I'm on the roam
my intent was always to come back home
then I lost my path and I lost my mind
and the way back home was so hard to find

Shelter

Underneath your wings
I will find rest and shelter
Safe from enemies

Your citadel walls
Are strong enough to repel
Those who wish me harm

You are my desire
You deliver me from fear
You give me freedom

NB: This poem consists of 3 haiku incorporated together into a narrative

Crimson Stain

How much hurt do you leave behind
when you walk away, and you've been unkind?
How many hearts lay scattered there
in acrimonious disrepair?
The words of hurt fly home to roost
and just as easily, they are loosed
a soul to injure or to maim
Indelible, the crimson stain

How many insults screamed out loud?
The vile oaths, the threatening vows?
How can mere words bring so much pain?
Why do they so much hurt sustain?
The nails are hammered into wood
the cryptic clues misunderstood
The nails pulled out, but holes remain
Indelible, the crimson stain

A slave is beaten, sold in chains
The master shouts his harsh refrains
History repeats, it never hears
The master never tastes the tears
Try as he might he'll never rinse
Those stains made by his fingerprints
His conscience never clear again
Indelible, the crimson stain

A child is orphaned by the war
Her life is shattered to the core
She wanders lonely streets alone
Forever where the winds have blown
The scars of conflict never fade
The pain of loss is retrograde
The horror seared into her brain
Indelible, the crimson stain

On mount Golgotha's ugly hill
Messiah hangs in silence still
Our weight of guilt laid on His back
as noon day skies turn darkest black
The price is paid for humankind
as God and nature realign
The blood flows from the open veins
Indelible, the crimson stain

Colour Chart

Violet and purple,
are the colours of despair
Scarlet and amber,
when danger plays its part
Platinum and blonde,
are the colours of her hair
Blue of deepest tincture,
is the colour of my heart

Dangerous Obsession

Drawn to the open flame
a dancing tongue of fire
Sucked in by radiant beauty
a primitive desire

Compulsive interaction
by heat and light seduced
Decaying orbits circling
until to ash reduced

Spongiform

I read more stories
than I could ever write
I imagine more battles
than I could ever fight
I sleep more dreams
than I could ever say
Like a sponge I soak up
each and every day

I absorb more knowledge
than I could ever show
I go to more places
than I should ever go
I write more scenes
than I could ever play
I soak up the hours
and I mop up the day

High and Dry

High and dry, I'm washed up
on the literary shore
Stranded on the rocks now
I'm not writing any more
My thoughts sleep on the shelf
gathering dust inside my mind
No more originality
my creativity in a bind

This shipwrecked poet signals
from a desert island knoll
Please come and rescue me,
my isolation took atoll
On an island in this ocean
I've no means of an escape
I cannot write my verses
I can't visualise their shape

I'm a castaway creative
and I die of poetic thirst
or I may die in obscurity
I don't know which is worse
No one reads my poetry
No-one it seems could care
It's so demotivational and
that's why my cupboard's bare

I'm high and dry, I'm stranded
on this literary beach
Creative thought has flown me,
it's been stolen from my reach
Inspiration has departed
My muse is here no more
Now this lyricist is washed up
on a barren rocky shore

Endgame

It doesn't take a Herculean effort
to see that life on this fragile blue planet
is becoming precarious and more than it
can contain is coming down on it
as nature writhes around in a febrile fit
while we transform each forest into a barren desert
and there seems no easy way of stopping it
as each corporation grasps for its share of the profit
we see the loud mouthed social media misfits
and hear all the political spin prophets
selling their souls on the back of it
and looking away from change in the climate
as they continue to deny there's anything in it

This is more than a tragic shame
and we all need to take the blame
rich and poor, all of us are just the same
no excuses, whether justified or lame
we just sold our planet down the lane
when we took our eyes off the ball in the game
and our children's futures are running down the drain
as we start the countdown for this planet's endgame

We have long been abusing our tenure
when we think we can do what we want here
but as the sea levels rise dangerously higher
and destructive storms become increasingly stronger
and drought and floods are an imminent danger
the odds are becoming so much longer
as we try to prolong our collective survival
our carbon emissions stand without rival

and you know this stuff is far from trivial
though the will to stop it ain't controversial
but all of the top climate change deniers

and the myriad ignorant science decriers
conveniently overlook all the facts in the files
they're fiddling while the earth is on fire
like Nero did as Rome's flames burnt higher
every last one of them is an absolute liar
each one is a self-interested betrayer
all part of a cabal of elite conspirers
hell bent on taking this down to the wire
while the Earth sits upon its own funeral pyre
and the future for our children is critically dire
and the world's population is foundering in the mire

We're living in a world of torment
where we all of us could easily prevent
the world's next extinction level event
if only we would mutually consent
to limit the rubbish we have sent
up into the sky and the firmament
we know the atmosphere is not infinite
and our resources were never permanent
but the population seems to be hell bent
on a global scenario involving detriment

The exponential rise in killer diseases
signals imminent destruction of our species
and while our survival chance decreases
it's likely we'll see the mass decimation

of our society in this next generation
with industrialised total domination
and ecological saturation
through the wanton, thoughtless jeopardization
of the health and safety of the population
This is more than a tragic shame
and each of us need to accept this blame
rich and poor, we're all in this the same
there can be no excuses, whether justified or lame
for the way humanity has played this game
we collectively sold this planet down the lane
each of us has initiated this planet's endgame

The Last Laugh

I'll tell the jokes
and you wear your frown
I'll make them happy
when you bring them down
You play the straight man
and I'll act the clown
and I'll have the last laugh tonight

I'll bring the sunshine
when you bring the cloud
You fight your demons
while I please the crowd
I'll be the wedding
and you be the shroud
but I'll have the last laugh tonight

I'll write the comedy
you load your gun
You bring the sadness
but I'll have the fun
You'll stop the music
yet I won't succumb
'cos I'll have the last laugh tonight

Oh yeah
I'll have the last laugh tonight

If you enjoyed this book, you may also enjoy reading other titles recently published by Wheelsong Books:

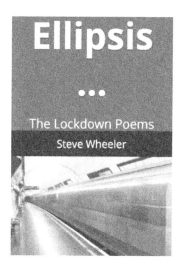

Ellipsis – The Lockdown Poems by Steve Wheeler

ISBN: 9-798666-415252

Poems written during the global pandemic of 2020 with themes ranging from heroism, depression, hope, racism and faith.

Inspirations – Poems and reflections by Kenneth Wheeler

ISBN: 9-798667-258360

Inspiration writing about faith, love, family, life and celebration of all things good. Proceeds go to Open Doors charity.

Sacred – Poems by Steve Wheeler

ISBN: 9-798669-576806

A collection of poems charting the author's journey of faith, and exploring love, hope, failure, fear, redemption, poverty and racism.

Urban Voices – Poems by Steve Wheeler

ISBN: 9-798692-556097

A collection of new poems about city life, contains dark, wry and ironic observations on urban life, identity, crime and poverty.

All titles are available for purchase in paperback and Kindle editions on Amazon.com or direct from the publisher.

Printed in Great Britain
by Amazon

65602016R00078